COOKING FOR TWO
Your Cat & You!

For all the cool cats.

COOKING FOR TWO
Your Cat & You!

*Delicious Recipes for You and
Your Favorite Feline*

*By Brandon Schultz
& Lucy Schultz-Osenlund*

SKYHORSE PUBLISHING

Visit our website at www.skyhorsepublishing.com.

10 9 8 7 6 5 4 3 2 1

Library of Congress Cataloging-in-Publication Data is available on file.

Cover design by R. Kurt Osenlund
Cover photo credit Brandon Schultz and iStock
Interior cat images by iStock. Recipe images by Brandon Schultz.

Print ISBN: 978-1-63220-461-5
Ebook ISBN: 978-1-63450-964-0

Printed in China

Dogs eat. Cats dine. —ANN TAYLOR

TABLE OF CONTENTS

A NOTE ON INGREDIENTS

As with any recipe, you should feel free to adapt ingredients and methods as your tastes and experience allow. **Unlike** most recipes, you're cooking these for your feline family, too. Many foods that are innocuous to humans can be toxic to cats in certain quantities, and some ingredients may be fatal at any dosage. Please familiarize yourself with the list below, and never add anything from the No-No list to any part of the meal that your kitty will consume!

Though some of these can be consumed in very small quantities, it's better to be safe than sorry. With very few exceptions, the recipes in this book avoid even those ingredients that are only dangerous at high dosage, and the exceptions are clearly noted. I strongly recommend you do **not** add any quantity of these ingredients on your own when making alterations to the recipes for kitty, and I urge you only to adapt recipes for humans!

Like a human fingerprint, each cat's nose pad has a unique pattern.

NO-NO LIST

Just Don't Do It!

Avocado

Chocolate

Cinnamon (very small doses okay)

Citrus fruit or juice

Coffee (including grounds)

Fat (don't let kitty eat fat trimmings while preparing meals)

Fruit—see the note at the bottom of the page

Garlic

Grapes

Mushroom

Nutmeg (very small doses okay)

Nuts (especially macadamia)

Raisin

Salt (in excess, so don't add it!)

Sugar (in excess, so don't add it!)

Tea (including leaves/herbs)

Tomato (especially green, and the greens from the plant)

A SPECIAL NOTE ABOUT FRUIT

Most fruits (aside from grapes) are okay for cats, but the seeds (apples, pears) and pits (apricots, cherries) are potentially toxic, so be sure your cat only has access to the flesh of the fruits you provide! If you're unsure about a particular fruit, the ASPCA* provides an extensive, online list of plants and fruits that are potentially dangerous, so check it out before offering anything new to your cat!

*http://www.aspca.org/pet-care/animal-poison-control/toxic-and-non-toxic-plants

In the middle of a world that had always been a bit mad, the cat walks with confidence.
— Rosanne Amberson

A Note on Milk

Cats and milk form a natural pair in our minds, but they are not always so great together in reality. While most kittens tolerate (and love!) milk and dairy products, many cats develop some level of lactose intolerance as they age. It's the same with humans: Some of us stop producing the enzyme lactase as we get older and don't need birth milk any more, so we have difficulty digesting the lactose in milk. Over time, your cat should learn if milk upsets him, and he'll shy away from dairy products naturally, but some cats find the habit hard to kick even when it hurts.

Look out for vomiting or, more likely, diarrhea 8–12 hours after dairy consumption. If this happens regularly, it's a pretty sure bet that your kitty can't digest lactose anymore, and you should stop giving him milk. Don't worry, he's not going to develop anything fatal from milk consumption. However, no one likes a stomachache, so help him out by keeping dairy out of reach on a regular basis.

Not all dairy is created equal, though. Even if your cat can't handle milk well, chances are he can tolerate some other dairy products that are often cultured (so some of the lactose has been eaten away), like cheeses and yogurt products.

If your cat turns out to be lactose intolerant, skip milk anywhere it appears in the book, and substitute water or chicken stock as you see fit. I've tried to keep the milk to a minimum anyway, so you'll be fine!

SNACKS & SIDES

SPINACH & QUINOA SIDE SALAD

Ingredients

FOR BOTH
2 ½ cups fresh spinach
   leaves
1 cup cooked quinoa*
   (any variety, but red or
   tricolor will look best!)
¾ cup crumbled feta

FOR HUMANS
Extra virgin olive oil
Balsamic vinegar
Coarse ground sea salt

Preparation

FOR HUMANS
1. Add spinach to a salad bowl and drizzle olive oil over the
   leaves.
2. Top with the cooked quinoa and sprinkle feta over salad.
3. Splash the balsamic vinegar on top, and finish with the coarse
   ground sea salt if desired.

FOR CATS
1. Remove excess stems and chop the spinach into medium
   pieces, then add to a cat bowl.
2. Top with cooked quinoa and sprinkle with a small amount of
   well-crumbled feta.

COOKED QUINOA*

Quinoa is generally cooked at a 2:1 liquid:quinoa ratio. Your quinoa will be more flavorful if you use chicken broth instead of water for at least half of the liquid. I use it for all 2 cups! (Make sure to use pure chicken broth without seasonings like onion or garlic powders since kitty is eating this!)

KITTY NOT INTERESTED?

Add a spritz of pure chicken broth as a dressing and toss before trying again!

Cats are master manipulators! A 2009 study showed that kitties develop an exaggerated purr–cry that humans can't resist, and they only employ it against their own humans. When do they use it? When they want food, of course!

If man could be crossed with the cat it would improve the man, but it would deteriorate the cat.
—MARK TWAIN

A cat has 230 bones, compared to a human's 206.

PUMPKIN SOUP

Ingredients

FOR BOTH
2 cups chicken broth
1 teaspoon ground ginger
½ teaspoon ground paprika
1 cup pumpkin puree
¼ cup heavy whipping
    cream
Sour cream for garnish

FOR HUMANS
Pepper
Ground Cinnamon

Preparation

1. Heat the chicken stock in a covered pot until it begins to simmer.
2. Add the ginger and paprika, and stir until blended. Whisk away any clumps.
3. Add the pumpkin puree and bring the soup to a boil.
4. Reduce the heat to a simmer, cover, and cook for 15 minutes, stirring occasionally.
5. Add the whipping cream and stir to blend. Continue cooking to heat through, but do not allow the soup to boil (about 2 minutes)!

FOR HUMANS
1. Ladle into a soup bowl and top with pepper as desired, a sprinkle of cinnamon, and a dollop of sour cream

FOR CATS
1. Ladle about half of a cup into a small bowl and top with a dollop of sour cream. Be sure to let your cat's soup cool from hot to warm before serving!

TIP!

Ladle your cat's serving first, then let it sit uncovered to cool for a few minutes. The small portion should cool quickly. When kitty's serving is cool enough, reheat your pot of soup before dishing out your own portion so yours can still be nice and hot! Save the sour cream for both until just before serving!

KITTY NOT INTERESTED?

Many cats who are excited by people food are less adventurous with liquids, so kitty may not care to slurp up a bowl of soup. If that's the case, try drizzling a little over her dry food—but don't turn the bowl into a soup! Skip the sour cream in this case.

"What's your name," Coraline
asked the cat. "Look, I'm
Coraline. Okay?"
"Cats don't have names," it said.
"No?" said Coraline.
"No," said the cat. "Now you
people have names. That's
because you don't know who
you are. We know who we are,
so we don't need names."
—NEIL GAIMAN, *CORALINE*

How do cats always hear the crack of a can opening from anywhere in the house? It doesn't hurt that their ears can pivot 180° each, giving them 360° of surround sound at any time!

Cats never strike a pose that
isn't photogenic.
—LILLIAN JACKSON BRAUN

CHICKEN SOUP WITH CARROTS

Your cat always comforts you when you're sick, so why not reward your feline nurse with some of your chicken noodle soup?

Ingredients

FOR BOTH
6 cups chicken broth, made from chicken bouillon*
1 pound chicken (your favorite parts), chopped
1 small bundle fresh parsley, tied (about ten stems)
½ cup grated or finely chopped carrots (about 4 medium carrots)
½ cup heavy cream

FOR HUMANS
1 cup egg noodles, cooked
Salt and pepper to taste

Preparation

1. Heat the water and chicken bouillon over medium-high heat until the bouillon is fully absorbed.
2. Set aside two stems of parsley. Add the rest to the pot (still tied), along with the chopped chicken, and cook for 8 minutes.
3. Add the carrots and cook for an additional 10 minutes, stirring occasionally.
4. Remove the tied parsley from the pot and discard. Chop the leaves of the two reserved parsley stems and add it to the pot.
5. Add the heavy cream, stir, and serve!

FOR HUMANS
1. Add the noodles to your individual bowl. These add little to no nutritional value for kitty, so they're just for you!
2. Add salt and pepper as desired.

FOR CATS
1. Ladle about half a cup of soup into a small bowl and let it cool before serving.

CHICKEN BOUILLON*

Follow your bouillon package's instructions to reach 6 cups of finished broth. Make sure the bouillon you purchase doesn't contain onion or garlic (including powders) in its ingredients! If you can't find any, you can use a pure chicken stock.

TIP!

Ladle your cat's serving first, then let it sit uncovered to cool for a few minutes. The small portion should cool quickly. When kitty's serving is cool enough, reheat your pot of soup before dishing out your own portion so yours can still be nice and hot!

KITTY NOT INTERESTED?

Try adding a teeny bit more heavy cream to the top of your cat's portion and not mixing it in. The smell of the cream may whet her appetite, and the taste of the chicken should keep her excited once she gets started. Don't be insulted if she doesn't lap up all the broth. Most kitties aren't as adventurous with liquids as they are with solids!

If you're reading this book, chances are you're an ailurophile. Ailurophilia is the love of cats!

What greater gift than the love of a cat.
—CHARLES DICKENS

STEAMED GREEN BEANS

Green beans, recommended by the ASPCA as a safe snack for cats, are especially useful as a substitute for unhealthy packaged treats. If you have a treat lover who needs to lose a couple pounds, green beans are an excellent alternative snack and, unlike human children, cats tend to love their greens! Be sure to strictly control your cat's portions here, though, as too many vegetables can have a negative effect on his digestion and ability to absorb nutrients. Just a few will do the trick!

Ingredients

FOR BOTH
1 large handful of fresh
   green beans

FOR HUMANS
1 teaspoon vegetable oil
3–4 garlic cloves, sliced
   thin (or more if you love
   garlic!)
1 Tablespoon olive oil
1 teaspoon lemon juice
Coarse ground sea salt

Preparation

1. Rinse the green beans and pat them dry with a paper towel. Trim the hard edges and stems with a knife or kitchen scissors.
2. Bring water to a boil in a steamer. Add the green beans and steam for 5 minutes, until tender but not completely limp. Remove them from the steamer and cool, uncovered. Set aside 4–5 beans (3–4 if they are particularly long) for your cat.

FOR HUMANS
1. While the beans are cooling, heat the vegetable oil over medium-high heat, then sauté the sliced garlic until lightly browned, about 2–3 minutes.
2. Add the beans to the pan and reheat with the garlic.

3. Remove the beans and garlic to a small bowl and toss in the olive oil.
4. Add the lemon juice and toss again.
5. Sprinkle with sea salt.

FOR CATS
1. Your cat's beans are healthiest completely undressed. If they are large/long, cut them in half before serving.

TIP!

Some believe that olive oil can aid digestion in cats. If you want to coat kitty's beans, be sure to use less than a teaspoon. Too much can cause diarrhea.

KITTY NOT INTERESTED?

If your cat's a little leery of the long beans, or he's having trouble chewing them, mash them to a mushier consistency. He doesn't care about presentation!

According to Herodotus, some ancient Egyptians would shave their eyebrows in mourning when a household cat died! Even more extreme, killing a cat (even accidentally) could incur the death penalty, and Egyptian men would guard fires to ensure that no cat could accidentally run into one.

The 9th century BC saw the rise of Bast, the Egyptian cat goddess whose cult drew thousands of pilgrims annually to the city of Bubastis. She represented fertility, motherhood, and protection. The cult held prominence for almost 1400 years before being officially banned in 390 AD.

I believe cats to be spirits come to earth.
A cat, I am sure, could walk on a cloud
without coming through.
—JULES VERNE

REAL POPCORN

Popcorn is a delicious human treat that has been around for centuries, and *real* popcorn can be enjoyed by your cat, too! Skip packaged, microwaveable popcorn full of questionable ingredients. You'd be better off without this product yourself, but your cat definitely shouldn't have it. Buy kernels and make this snack at home on the stovetop. It's so simple and delicious you'll wonder why you haven't been doing this all along!

Ingredients

FOR BOTH
3 Tablespoons peanut oil
(or any oil with a high
smoke point, like canola
oil)
⅓ cup popcorn kernels

FOR HUMANS
2–3 Tablespoons butter
Seasonings, your favorites
(everything tastes good
on popcorn)

Preparation

1. Heat the oil in a large pan over medium-high heat.
2. Add a few test kernels and cover.
3. When the test kernels pop, remove the pan from the heat, and add the remaining kernels. Wait thirty seconds, then return the pan to the heat and cover. When the kernels begin popping, tilt the lid slightly to allow steam to escape.
4. Shake the pan gently while the kernels pop. This process will be quick, as the kernels should all pop together.
5. Remove to a large serving bowl. Set aside a very small handful for kitty.

FOR HUMANS
1. Microwave the butter for 10–15 seconds to melt it. Add seasonings, and allow the mixture to cool for at least one minute (or your popcorn will shrivel from the hot butter), then pour the mixture over popcorn and toss gently.

FOR CATS

1. Do not butter or salt your cat's popcorn at all. No seasonings are necessary, and some may be harmful, so give your cat plain popcorn and let her enjoy. She may spend most of her time playing with it, and only nibbling small pieces. Consider this a bonus—a treat and a toy all in one!

SUGGESTIONS!

Need some popcorn flavoring ideas for *your* share? Try sprinkling these on your hot, buttered popcorn:
- Grated Parmesan cheese and dried basil
- Garlic salt and dried oregano
- Brown sugar and cinnamon
- Sea salt and vinegar (skip the butter with this one!)
- Cracked black pepper and dried rosemary
- Paprika and onion powder
- Ranch seasoning packet
- Taco seasoning packet

BRUNCH

SWEET POTATO OMELET

Ingredients

FOR BOTH
6 small eggs
3 Tablespoons butter
1 cup finely diced sweet
    potato
1 cup shredded cheddar
    cheese
Dried thyme

FOR HUMANS
¼ cup thinly sliced onion
Salt and pepper

Preparation

1. Blanch* the sweet potato chunks for 3 minutes.
2. Melt 1 Tablespoon of butter in a small frying pan over medium heat and cook the sweet potatoes for 7 minutes, stirring occasionally. Separate into two bowls, with ¾ of the potato in one, and the remaining ¼ in the other.
3. Cook the onions in the pan until softened, about 2 minutes. Add more butter if needed. Add cooked onion to the ¾ portion of sweet potato.
4. Beat the eggs in a small mixing bowl, add dried thyme, and set aside.

FOR CATS
1. Melt 1 Tablespoon of butter in a medium frying pan.
2. Pour about one quarter of the eggs (err on the side of too little, rather than too much) into the pan and cook until the eggs are nearly finished.
3. Add the ¼ portion of sweet potato (onion-free!) and half of the cheddar cheese to one half of the pan, fold the empty half of the egg over the vegetables with a spatula, and continue cooking to desired consistency.
4. Remove to a plate, cut into small kitty-size bites, and allow to cool.

FOR HUMANS

1. Complete steps 1–3 above using the remaining eggs and the sweet potato/onion mixture in step 3.
2. Cut in half, garnish with salt and pepper to taste, and serve!

BLANCH*

Blanching is a technique that pre-cooks a vegetable and immediately stops the freezing process through cold shocking. Prepare a bath of ice water in a large bowl, then bring a pot of water to a rolling boil. Drop the vegetables into the boiling water for the directed amount of time (in this case, 3 minutes), then immediately transfer them to the ice bath (a slotted spoon works well for this) for 1 minute. Drain the water, pat the vegetables dry with a paper towel, then allow to air-dry further if necessary.

A cat has absolute emotional honesty:
human beings, for one reason or another,
may hide their feelings, but a cat does not.
— ERNEST HEMINGWAY

Cats are only awake for about $\frac{1}{3}$ of their lives, and they spend an average of $\frac{1}{3}$ of their waking hours cleaning themselves! That leaves just about only 20 percent of their lives for playing and for eating, so make it count!

I love cats because I enjoy
my home; and little by little,
they become its visible soul.
—JEAN COCTEAU

SPINACH & FETA FRITTATA

Frittatas can be made with just about any ingredients baked among eggs. Once you master the frittata, have fun experimenting with different ingredients for yourself, but this delicious recipe is safe to share with kitty!

Ingredients

FOR BOTH
1 Tablespoon vegetable oil
2 cups fresh spinach, ribboned*
8 eggs
1 Tablespoon dried basil
1 Tablespoon butter
¾ cup crumbled feta

FOR HUMANS
Basil leaves for garnish
Salt and pepper

Preparation

1. Preheat the oven to 375°F.
2. Heat the vegetable oil in a medium pan over medium-high heat.
3. Add the spinach and stir constantly until it begins to turn bright green and starts to wilt, about 2 minutes. Remove to a plate.
4. Beat the eggs in a medium mixing bowl and add dried basil, stirring to combine.
5. Melt the butter in the pan over medium heat, increase the heat to medium-high, and add the eggs to the pan.
6. Distribute the spinach and feta evenly throughout the pan, and cook until the edge of the eggs begins to solidify, about 2–3 minutes.
7. Add whole basil leaves to the parts you will eat, and leave the cat's portion unadorned. While garnishing, keep in mind the finished product will be cut like a pizza.
8. Transfer the pan to the center rack of the oven, and cook 10–12 minutes, until the egg reaches a puffy texture. It's fine to cook this a few minutes shorter or longer if you have strong egg-consistency preferences.
9. Remove from the oven, transfer to a cutting surface, and slice like a pizza.

FOR HUMANS

1. Season with salt and pepper as needed and enjoy!

FOR CATS

1. Cut your cat's portion into tiny bite-size pieces and allow it to cool before serving. Remember to serve her pieces without whole basil leaves on top! (Basil is okay for kitty, but whole pieces are a potential choking hazard.)

RIBBONED*

Ribboning is simply cutting leaves into thin strips. You can stack several leaves before slicing with the point of a sharp knife to speed up the process.

TIP!

If you're using a frying pan that has a plastic handle, you'll want to wrap the handle completely with aluminum foil before transferring to the oven. Most silicone handles are safe up to at least 400°F, but you can wrap any handle if it makes you feel better!

Cat brains are more similar to human brains than they are to dog brains, especially regarding emotion receptors.

There is, incidentally, no way of talking about cats that enables one to come off as a sane person.
—DAN GREENBERG

While a human pregnancy lasts about 9 months and usually produces one child, a cat pregnancy lasts around 9 weeks and will generally produce 1–9 kittens.

SCRAMBLED EGGS WITH RICE

Ingredients

FOR BOTH
6 eggs
1 Tablespoon butter
⅓ cup cooked rice

FOR HUMANS
¼ cup shredded cheddar
  cheese
Salt and pepper

Preparation

1. Beat the eggs in a small mixing bowl.
2. Melt the butter in a small frying pan over medium-high heat.
3. Reduce the heat to medium-low and add the eggs and rice, spreading the rice evenly.
4. Cook slowly over low heat, stirring in small circles often, preferably with a whisk.*
5. When the eggs are *almost* the consistency you prefer, remove the pan from the flame, separate ⅔ of the eggs in the pan, and add the shredded cheese to this portion. Remove the eggs from the pan immediately, keeping the two portions separated. (The cheese will melt as the eggs finish cooking off the flame.)

FOR HUMANS
1. To the cheesy eggs, add salt and pepper to taste. Not only shouldn't you add this to kitty's portion at all, but you should never add salt to eggs until they're finished anyway, or they'll dry out.

FOR CATS
1. Allow to cool before serving.

*TIP!

Whisking the eggs in small circles while cooking results in tinier curds, which are better for your cat to chew. You might prefer larger curds in your scrambled eggs (which can be achieved with spatula, using a sweeping motion instead of whisking or stirring) but this isn't the best technique for serving kitty.

SPECIAL TREAT FOR KITTY!

If your cat tolerates cheese, feel free to sprinkle a few shreds into hers before allowing it to cool. There's no reason she can't have a little if she can digest it, and she'll enjoy it.

SPECIAL TREAT FOR YOU!

If eggs and rice is a little too bland for your morning, add a small topping of salsa to liven it up, and serve it on a piece of buttered toast! No salsa for kitty, though.

The cat could very well be man's
best friend but would never stoop
to admitting it.
—DOUG LARSON

In the 1960s, the CIA spent over $20 million training cats to spy on the Soviets.

As every cat owner knows,
nobody owns a cat.
—ELLEN PERRY BERKELEY

FRIED EGGS & HAM

A protein-packed breakfast for a busy day of lots of play (and a few naps!).

Ingredients

FOR BOTH
1 Tablespoon vegetable oil
1 ham steak
1 Tablespoon butter
3 eggs

FOR HUMANS
Maple syrup and hot sauce,
    optional
Salt and pepper, to taste

Preparation

1. Heat the vegetable oil in a medium pan over medium-high heat.
2. Add the ham steak to the oil and cook two minutes, flip, and repeat until steak is lightly browned and done (if you're using a meat thermometer, the ham steak should reach 145°F). Total cooking time should be between 10 and 15 minutes, depending on the thickness of the steak. Remove to a plate.
3. In a medium pan, melt the butter over medium heat. Reduce heat to the lowest possible setting when the butter is melted but not yet crackling or browning.
4. Crack the eggs onto a plate, then slide them gently into the melted butter. Cover*, and cook until the whites appear creamy white and the yolks just start to firm around the edges, approximately 4–5 minutes.

FOR CATS
1. Top a small piece of ham steak with one fried egg and dice in kitty-size bites.
2. The dish should be cool enough to serve immediately, but test it with the back of your finger first. Allow it to cool an extra minute if it's still hot.

FOR HUMANS

1. Top your serving of ham steak with hot maple syrup, if desired (just heat some up in the microwave for ten seconds!).
2. Add two fried eggs and top with salt, pepper, and a dash of hot sauce, if desired.

TIP*

Covering the eggs while cooking traps the steam to cook both sides of the egg simultaneously without flipping the eggs and potentially breaking them!

YOUR CALL!

I prefer to cook my cat's egg an extra thirty seconds or so until the yolk firms up a bit more. Aside from salmonella, raw egg can lead to skin and coat issues for kitties, as it may decrease vitamin B absorption!

Kittens are born with their eyes shut. They open them in about six days, take a look around, then close them again for the better part of their lives.
—Stephen Baker

OATMEAL WITH BERRIES

Steel cut oats take longer to cook than the more common rolled oats, but the thicker texture and potential health benefits make them worth the wait. Experiment with the water ratio to create thicker or creamier outcomes until you find your favorite!

Ingredients

FOR BOTH
1 cup steel cut oats
3 cups water
Handful of blueberries and
    strawberries

FOR HUMANS
Other berries, if preferred
Maple syrup
Cinnamon
Crushed walnuts, if desired

Preparation

1. Add the oats and water to a small pot and bring to a boil over medium-high heat.
2. Reduce the heat to low, cover, and cook until the water is absorbed, about 20 minutes.*
3. When the oats are finished, remove any film that may have formed over the surface, and stir.

FOR CATS
1. Mash a few blueberries and a strawberry, and add to about ½ cup of cooled oatmeal in a small bowl.

FOR HUMANS
1. Add maple syrup and a healthy amount of cinnamon to your serving, and mix thoroughly.
2. Top with a sprinkle of cinnamon, a handful of berries, and crushed walnuts if desired.

Don't worry if your cooking time varies, even dramatically. Depending on your heat source, your water may absorb at very different speeds. If the water is gone very quickly and the oats are still too firm, add more water and try to reduce your heat as much as possible. You're looking for a very low setting.

CAUTION: You're free to add any berries you love to *your* oatmeal, but don't experiment with kitty's. Blueberries and strawberries are safe for cats in small portions, but other berries (like blackberries) can cause allergic reactions or be dangerous to their systems. Go wild with yours, but play it safe with kitty's.

Stubbs has been the honorary mayor of Talkeetna, Alaska, since July 1997, serving eighteen years at the time of this printing. Stubbs is a cat, and shares a birthday with Lucy, the coauthor of this book!

DELI ROLLUPS

These simple snacks take little seasoning and are just as delicious to kitty as they are to you! Feel free to use your favorite lean deli meats instead of what's suggested below, but don't let kitty have any that are seasoned.

Ingredients

FOR BOTH
1 cup basil leaves
¼ cup grated Parmesan cheese
¼ cup olive oil
4 slices lean turkey breast
4 slices lean chicken breast
4 slices lean ham
3 ounces cream cheese, softened

Preparation

Before you start: Be sure your cream cheese is soft (room temperature) or it'll tear your meats. To speed up the process, microwave the cream cheese for 20 seconds. If it's still too hard to spread easily, repeat for 5 seconds at a time until it's ready!

1. Prepare a pesto spread by blending the basil and Parmesan cheese in a food processor and slowly adding the oil while the machine is on.
2. Stack two slices of each meat in pairs (turkey on turkey, etc.) so you have 6 stacks (two of each meat).
3. Spread the cream cheese, pesto, or both on the meats. (If your pesto is runny, you'll need a layer of cream cheese underneath to hold it all together.)
4. Roll the meats into tight logs.

FOR CATS
1. Slice off a few pieces of each type of meat for kitty.
2. Slice each piece into thin wheels.

DAIRY DILEMMA?

If your cat can't tolerate dairy, use only pesto, and prepare a thicker consistency. Without cream cheese underneath, you'll need to be sure the pesto doesn't drain out of the logs!

PESTO PRO

*If your pesto is extremely thick, add a little more oil and continue blending until it reaches a creamier consistency. You're not looking for a true sauce here, so it shouldn't be runny. You need it to be spreadable!

*Typical pesto would include garlic, pine nuts, and some salt. None of these are great for kitty, and garlic is potentially toxic, so don't include it!

Google's artificial brain project in the Google X lab consists of 16,000 processors with the freedom to study anything it wants on the Internet. It dwells on cat videos.

You probably have friends who are allergic to cats, but did you know cats are developing allergies to human lifestyle habits, like cigarette smoke, human dandruff, and house dust?

If animals could speak, the dog would be a
blundering outspoken fellow;
but the cat would have the rare grace of never
saying a word too much.
—MARK TWAIN

FRUIT SALAD

Ingredients*

FOR BOTH
Strawberries
Bananas
Apples, no seeds
Blueberries
Watermelon, no seeds

FOR HUMANS
Maple Syrup

Preparation

1. Chop your chosen fruits to your desired size.
2. Add all of the fruits to a mixing bowl and toss.

FOR CATS
1. Remove kitty's portion of fruit and chop it further if you left some fruits in large pieces. Your cat can bite through all of these, but it doesn't hurt to give her a hand.

FOR HUMANS
1. Drizzle some maple syrup on top of the remaining salad and toss to coat fruits. Don't overdo it—just enough for a little glisten, not a sticky glop!

INGREDIENTS*

You may notice there are no measurements here. This is a list of fruits that are both safe for cats and often enjoyed by them, so choose your favorites, and make yourselves a nice salad! If you use watermelon or apple, just be sure to remove all seeds, and make sure you use the fleshier parts of the apple rather than the harder parts close to the core.

Only about half of all cats have any sensitivity to catnip.

DINNER

ARROZ CON POLLO

A traditional preparation of this dish looks a bit different, but here's a healthy alternative that's safe to share with your cat!

Ingredients

FOR BOTH
1 Tablespoon vegetable oil
2 chicken thighs*
Salt and pepper
1 green bell pepper,
    chopped
2 cups chicken broth
1 cup rice*
1 cup peas
⅓ cup parsley, chopped

Preparation

1. In a large frying pan, heat the oil over medium-high heat.
2. Season the chicken thighs with salt and pepper.
3. Add the chicken thighs to the pan and brown on all sides, about 8–10 minutes. Remove to a plate.
4. Drain all but 1 Tablespoon of fat and juices from the pan, then return to the flame, reducing to medium-low, and adding the chopped green pepper. Cook until softened, about 5 minutes.
5. Add the chicken broth and bring to a simmer.
6. Add the rice, return the chicken to the pan, cover, and simmer until chicken and rice are cooked, about 20 minutes. Depending on the type of rice you used, you will have extra broth leftover; drain it!
7. Top with parsley.

FOR CATS
1. Make sure kitty doesn't get any skin (she doesn't need added salt) and chop her meat into bite size pieces for serving over the rice and vegetables.
2. Cool and serve.

FOR HUMANS
1. Season with more sea salt and cracked black pepper if desired.

CHICKEN THIGHS*

The chicken parts you use are up to you, and darker meat is going to give you a juicier, more flavorful meal, but aim for a meat volume equivalent to 2 thighs. Just remember not to give kitty any salt and pepper. If you're using drumsticks, an easy plan is to skip the seasoning on one, and give that to kitty! (Pictured here is a chicken breast for the human and shredded drumstick meat for kitty.)

RICE*

This recipe is often made with yellow rice, but you won't have much luck finding packaged yellow rice that your kitty can eat. Most contain onion and/or garlic. (Pictured here is a mix of white and brown rice.)

MIND YOUR PEAS!

If you're using frozen peas, rinse them in warm water to remove any ice chunks, and dry them on a paper towel before adding them to pan. You don't want frost to dilute your broth.

Why do you have to cut kitty's food into such small pieces? Cat jaws can't move sideways and they can't grind their teeth, so it's much more difficult to manage large bites.

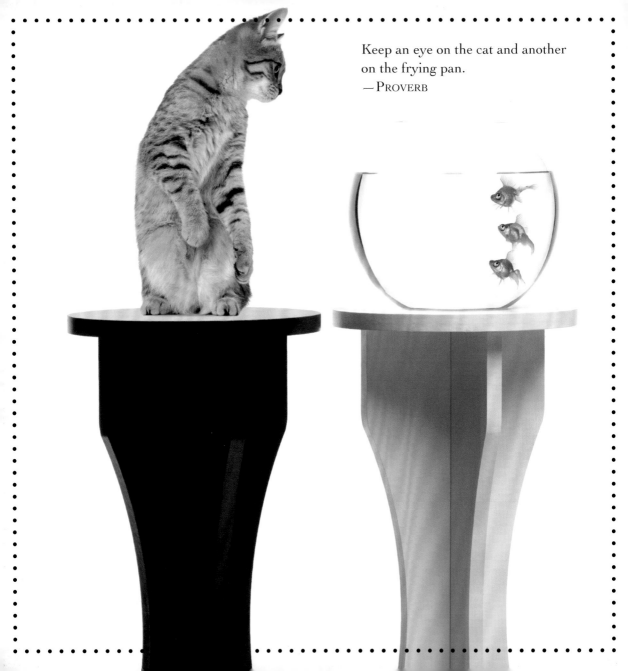

Keep an eye on the cat and another on the frying pan.
— PROVERB

A cat has 30 permanent teeth, but most of them are used primarily for grooming!

THANKSGIVING DINNER

Ingredients

FOR BOTH
1–2 turkey tenderloins
1 Tablespoon butter, softened
1 cup chicken broth
1 can jellied cranberry sauce
1 can whole corn kernels

FOR HUMANS
Gravy, if desired
Salt and pepper

Preparation

1. Preheat the oven to 400°F.
2. Rub the turkey with butter. If you're using more than one tenderloin, you can season one with salt and pepper, as long as you leave one plain for kitty.
3. Place the turkey in a greased baking dish, and add the chicken broth.
4. Bake until the turkey reaches an internal temperature of 165°F, approximately 25 minutes for one tenderloin, adding 5–7 minutes per additional tenderloin. Let a meat thermometer be the judge here.
5. Heat the corn in a small pot, covered, over medium-high heat for 3 minutes, stirring once.
6. Remove the jellied cranberry sauce from the can, and slice into thin medallions.

FOR CATS
1. Mash one thin medallion of cranberry sauce with a fork.
2. Cut half a turkey tenderloin into bite-size pieces. It should be an appropriate temperature by now, but allow it to cool further if it's still hot.
3. Add mashed cranberry, corn, and turkey to a small dish and serve!

FOR HUMANS
1. Top your turkey with gravy, or season with salt and pepper, if desired, and enjoy with cranberry sauce and corn!

KITTY NOT INTERESTED?

If your cat is leaving one or two ingredients untouched and you really want her to clean her plate, mix it all together into a nice mush and see if that helps. It's not pretty, but it's still yummy!

Have you ever wondered how the sofa can be completely covered in cat hair the day after you cleaned it and you brushed kitty? Cats have about 130,000 hairs per square inch! You'll never get it all.

I had been told that the training procedure with cats was difficult. It's not. Mine had me trained in two days.
—BILL DANA

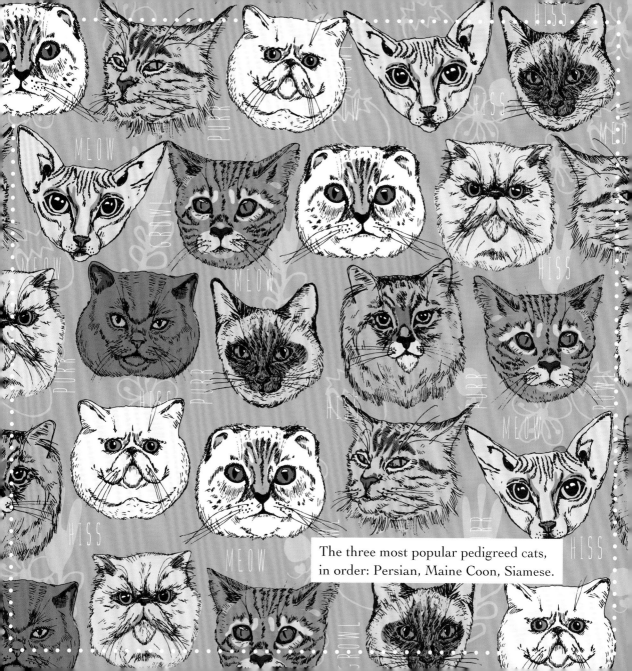

The three most popular pedigreed cats, in order: Persian, Maine Coon, Siamese.

TUNA SALAD

Cats famously love tuna, and it's safe for them eat in small quantities, but don't offer it frequently. In large doses, tuna can upset a cat's digestive system.

Ingredients

FOR BOTH
2 cans of white meat tuna in
    water (6 ounces each)
3 Tablespoons mayonnaise
3 Tablespoons finely
    chopped celery
1 Tablespoon finely
    chopped parsley
Bibb lettuce

FOR HUMANS
Salt and pepper

Preparation

1. In a mixing bowl, pull apart the drained tuna with a fork (or two).
2. Add the mayonnaise, celery, and parsley, and mix to combine. If it's too runny, add more tuna meat. Too thick? Add a little more mayo.

FOR CATS
1. Scoop about ⅓ cup of the tuna salad into a leaf of lettuce, and serve.

FOR HUMANS
1. Add salt and pepper to the remaining tuna salad and stir.
2. Cover a plate with a few leaves of lettuce and top with tuna salad.

SECONDS FOR KITTY!

If you plan to give kitty another serving tomorrow, refrigerate a small portion before adding the salt and pepper for your own plate. Cats shouldn't eat canned tuna often, so don't go overboard with the servings here, no matter how much she likes it.

MIX IT UP!

Turn this into a tuna salad platter for yourself by adding sliced vegetables like raw peppers, cucumbers, or red onion! To add a sweet touch, mix some relish into your salad, too!

A group of cats is called a clowder, and
a group of kittens is called a kindle.

You will always be lucky if you know
how to make friends with strange cats.
— PROVERB

You probably know
that a male cat is a
tom, but did you know
a female is a molly?

SALMON & STEAMED BROCCOLI

SALMON

Ingredients

FOR BOTH
2 Tablespoons + 2
   Tablespoons butter,
   divided
1 Tablespoon finely
   chopped tarragon
1 teaspoon dried basil
2 salmon fillets (about 6
   ounces each)

FOR HUMANS
1 lemon, halved

Preparation

1. Heat 2 Tablespoons of butter in the microwave for 10–15 seconds, until melted. Add the tarragon and basil to the butter and stir to combine. Coat the salmon fillets with the melted herb butter.
2. Heat the remaining 2 Tablespoons of butter in a medium pan over medium-high heat. Reduce the heat to medium and add the salmon fillets to the pan, cooking until lightly browned and the internal temperature reaches 145°F, about 4 minutes on each side.

FOR HUMANS
1. Serve with half of a lemon, to be squeezed over the salmon just before eating. Kitty only needs a small portion of the second fillet, so use the other half of your lemon when you eat the rest of her salmon!

FOR CATS
1. Allow the salmon to cool to room temperature and pull it apart into bite size pieces with a fork (or two!). Do not add lemon to kitty's meal. Lemon can be toxic to cats.

Ingredients

FOR BOTH
2 cups fresh broccoli

FOR HUMANS
2 Tablespoons butter
½ teaspoon garlic powder

Preparation

1. Bring water to a boil in a steamer.
2. Add broccoli and cook until bright green and tender (but not limp) when tested with a fork, about 5 minutes.

FOR CATS

1. Cool a few florets of broccoli and chop into bite-size pieces. Serve with no topping.

FOR HUMANS

1. Heat the butter in the microwave for 10–15 seconds, until melted.
2. Add the garlic powder, stir well to combine, and drizzle over your portion of broccoli.

SECONDS FOR KITTY!

If your cat is a broccoli fiend and is going to want seconds as a small snack later, put a couple pieces aside and refrigerate them before adding the garlic butter to your portion. Garlic is not safe for cats.

RRR
RRR

Researchers still don't know how cats purr.

Time spent with cats is never wasted.
— MAY SARTON

Cats can produce around 100 unique
sounds, but they use meowing almost
exclusively to communicate with humans.

MINI MEATLOAF & MASHED POTATOES

MEATLOAF

Ingredients

FOR BOTH
1 pound ground beef
1 egg
¼ cup diced green bell
   pepper
¼ cup unseasoned bread
   crumbs*
½ teaspoon salt
1 teaspoon black pepper

Preparation

1. Preheat the oven to 375°F.
2. In a large mixing bowl, add all of the ingredients and work through with your hands to combine.
3. Shape the mixture into a small loaf and add to a greased baking dish. Cook until a crust begins to form and the internal temperature is at least 160°F, about 50–60 minutes.
4. Allow the meatloaf to sit for at least 5 minutes before slicing.

FOR HUMANS
1. You may want to top your meatloaf with ketchup, steak sauce, or something similar. (None of these are okay for cats, as they contain tomato products, onion, and sometimes even garlic and raisin. Kitty just wants the beef anyway, so leave hers unadorned.)

FOR CATS
1. Use a fork to crumble kitty's portion, and allow it to cool before serving! Remember: no topping or seasoning!

BREADCRUMBS*

Most seasoned breadcrumbs include onion and garlic in some form, so it's safest to avoid seasoning altogether.

NO ONION?

No onion! Diced onion is a common ingredient in meatloaf, but it can be toxic to cats, so forego it this time! If you *must* have it, then break a very small serving of the beef mixture apart and set it aside before adding onions to the bulk. Form your loaf (with the onion) and kitty's small loaf separately. The cooking time will decrease for kitty's, so hers will probably be ready to come out of the oven after 20–25 minutes.

MASHED POTATOES

Ingredients

FOR BOTH

3–4 large russet potatoes, peeled and chopped into medium chunks

2 Tablespoons butter, softened

¼ cup sour cream

Splash of milk, if needed

FOR HUMANS

Salt and pepper

Preparation

1. Bring a large pot of water to a boil, reduce the heat to medium, add the potatoes, and cover loosely. Cook until a fork can slide into the potatoes without much resistance, but they don't fall apart, about 15–20 minutes, depending on the size of your chunks. Drain.
2. Add the butter and sour cream, and mix with a blender (creamier) or mash with a fork (chunkier), depending on your desired texture.
3. If your potatoes are too dry, add milk, a splash at a time, mixing until your desired consistency is reached.

FOR HUMANS

1. Season your portion with salt and pepper as desired, and maybe even a little more butter if you're feeling indulgent! Don't add anything to kitty's portion; there's already butter and sour cream in the recipe, so this isn't the most healthy meal for her to begin with. It's a treat, but don't go overboard!

The warmer the weather, the more cats breed. It's an angle of global warming you may not have considered!

People that don't like cats
haven't met the right one yet.
— DEBORAH A. EDWARDS

VEGETABLE STIR FRY

Ingredients

FOR BOTH
1 teaspoon canola oil
1 large handful fresh green
    beans, ends snipped
1 green bell pepper, sliced
1 large egg, beaten
¼ cup grated carrot
2 cups cooked rice

FOR HUMANS
1–2 teaspoons soy sauce
¼ inch fresh ginger*

Preparation

1. Heat a nonstick (or cast iron) pan over high heat until very hot. Add the oil, which should begin to smoke quickly.
2. Add the green beans and green pepper slices to the oil and stir continuously with a wooden spoon until the vegetables are tender, about 4–5 minutes.
3. Add the beaten egg and continue to stir constantly. The egg should break apart and begin to firm into many small pieces throughout the vegetables.
4. Add the carrot and the cooked rice, and toss to heat through.

FOR CATS
1. Remove a small portion to a bowl for kitty, cut any long vegetable pieces, and allow it to cool before serving.

FOR HUMANS
1. Add the desired amount of soy sauce to the pan.
2. Grate the ginger over the stir fry, and stir. Heat an additional minute, stirring constantly.
3. Garnish with a few large slices of ginger if you really enjoy this flavor!

MISSING SOMETHING?

If you love other ingredients in your stir fry, feel free to add them after you remove kitty's portion so you won't have to worry about what may harm her.

FRESH GINGER*

Grab one of those ugly roots of ginger next time you're in the produce section, stick it in a sealable bag, and pop it in the freezer. Ginger will keep for over a year, and it doesn't have to thaw before use. When you need it, wrap a paper towel around the base (so your hand doesn't freeze!), and use a potato peeler to shave fresh ginger into your dishes. You can peel the skin off the portion you're about to use first, but you don't even have to. The skin is edible.

SUCCESSFUL STIR FRY SECRETS

*The most important method for a successful stir fry is not to overcrowd the pan by cooking everything at once. Cook in stages, beginning with what takes longest to cook. We're not using any protein here, but if you want to, cook it first, remove it from the pan before cooking the vegetables, and add it back in with your rice at the end to warm it through briefly.

*Keep the pan hot, hot, hot! Cast iron is ideal for this, and American-made woks are not, as they don't usually hold heat well.

*Because your pan is so hot, stir constantly! You need to keep everything cooking, and nothing burning to the bottom of the pan!

Kitties eat grass to vomit intentionally. It helps rid their systems of any fur.

Cats with blue eyes are much
more likely to be deaf.

ROASTED PORK SHOULDER

Here's a no-fuss entree you can pair with any side for a hearty, comforting dinner!

Ingredients

FOR BOTH
3 Tablespoons olive oil
2 teaspoons dried oregano
1 teaspoon dried thyme
½ teaspoon black pepper
1 boneless pork shoulder*

Preparation

1. Preheat the oven to 450°F.
2. In a small bowl, mix the oil, oregano, thyme, and black pepper. Use a pastry brush to baste the pork shoulder with the seasoned oil.
3. Add the pork to a lightly greased roasting pan in the center of the oven, uncovered, and cook for 30 minutes.
4. Reduce the heat to 325°F and cook an additional 4 hours.
5. Remove the pork from the oven and allow it to sit at least 10 minutes before slicing.

FOR CATS
1. Cut a slice of pork into bite size pieces for kitty and allow it to cool before serving.

FOR HUMANS
1. You may want to top your pork with a finishing sauce or gravy, or simply top it with cracked black pepper and horseradish. It's up to you, just don't give kitty any toppings!

PORK SHOULDER*

A typical 4-pound shoulder will leave you with plenty of leftovers. If you don't want pork for days, get a 2-pounder. It doesn't affect cooking time.

WHAT ELSE?

You can serve this with any vegetables or sides you like for yourself, but if you want to include kitty, why not opt for a traditional potato and carrot combo for your roast? Chop potatoes into medium chunks and use baby carrots, adding them to your roasting pan about 30 minutes before the pork is finished, and you're all set!

You cannot look at a sleeping
cat and feel tense.
—LANE PAULEY

If your cat closes her eyes after she looks at you, it's a good sign, not a snub. Closed eyes generally mean that your kitty feels happy!

BAKED CHICKEN

There's nothing easier to bake than chicken, and your cat loves it as much as you do, so take a night off and treat yourselves to some simple home cooking!

Ingredients

FOR BOTH

2–3 pieces of your favorite chicken parts
2 Tablespoons olive oil
½ teaspoon salt
1 teaspoon black pepper

Preparation

1. Preheat the oven to 400°F.
2. In a small bowl, add the olive oil, salt, and pepper, and mix to combine.
3. With a pastry brush, coat the chicken parts thoroughly. Add more oil, as needed.
4. Arrange the chicken parts in a lightly greased baking dish with larger pieces toward the center, leaving plenty of room around each piece. Cook for 20–25 minutes to induce browning, then lower the temperature to 350°F and continue cooking an additional 20–30 minutes until the chicken is cooked completely (see Chicken Temperatures! below).
5. Remove the chicken from the oven, cover loosely with foil, and allow it to sit 10 minutes before serving.

FOR CATS

1. Kitty doesn't need the skin, so remove that and feel free to eat it yourself, or simply toss it. Cut kitty's portion into bite size pieces and allow it to cool before serving!

CHICKEN TEMPERATURES!

All chicken should reach at least 165°F for safety, but thighs and legs are often cooked to 175°F. Anything over 165°F and you're fine. You can also check that juices run clear (not pink) when the meat is cut.

WHAT ELSE?

Serve this with any vegetables or sides you like, but if you want to include kitty, rice makes a good bed for her chicken bites. Steamed green beans (see page 21) also go well with baked chicken!

DESSERT

VANILLA SUNDAE

Ingredients

FOR BOTH
Vanilla ice cream*
Whipped cream

FOR CATS
5 cat treats

FOR HUMANS
Chocolate syrup
Maraschino cherry
Crushed peanuts
Sprinkles
Anything!!

Preparation

FOR CATS
1. Add a small scoop of ice cream to a little bowl. (Truly, a small scoop.)
2. Top with a dollop of whipped cream.
3. Mash the cat treats into crumbs, then sprinkle them on the sundae. These are kitty-friendly sprinkles!

FOR HUMANS
1. You know how to do this. Throw a few scoops of ice cream into a bowl, and top it with all of your favorite human treats!

VANILLA ICE CREAM*

Vanilla is the safest choice for cats. If you can't stand it, give yourself something else, but give kitty vanilla. If your cat can't do dairy, try an alternative like soy-based ice cream! You'll want to skip the whipped cream topping, too, if this is the case. The crumbled cat treats will more than make up for it!

BE SELFISH, PLEASE!

There aren't really any sundae toppings kitty should have (chocolate, nuts, extra sugar, and chemicals are even worse for her than they are for you!), so make sure she doesn't get any on her sundae. Go to town with yours, but be responsible with hers! Eat it all yourself—you're doing her a favor!

Cats can hear ultrasonic sounds that rodents use to communicate. Humans and dogs can't hear them.

Cats know how to obtain food without labor, shelter without confinement, and love without penalties.
—W. L. George

Cats need $\frac{1}{6}$ the amount of light humans need to see clearly.

APPLE COBBLER

This delicious recipe is for two mini cobblers, and is designed for personal-size baking dishes, which you can pick up for a few dollars at any home goods store. If you'd rather use a standard pie dish, multiply the ingredients by four, and bake a little longer, until all of your apples are soft!

Ingredients

FOR BOTH
1 red delicious apple, peeled and sliced
1 granny smith apple, peeled and sliced
2 scant Tablespoons white sugar
1 scant Tablespoon brown sugar
2 Tablespoons flour
3 Tablespoons butter + more for greasing
1 pinch baking soda
1 pinch baking powder
3 heaping Tablespoons rolled oats

FOR HUMANS
Cinnamon

Preparation

1. Preheat the oven to 350°F.
2. In a medium bowl, add the apple slices, white sugar, brown sugar, and flour, and mix thoroughly.
3. Grease the baking dishes with butter generously, then arrange the apple slices evenly between them.
4. Heat the butter in the microwave for 10–15 seconds, until melted.
5. In the same mixing bowl, add the baking soda, baking powder, oats, and butter, and stir to combine.
6. Pour the topping evenly over the apples.
7. Bake until the apples are tender, about 20–30 minutes (30–40 for a full pie dish).

FOR CATS
1. Scoop a few spoonfuls of the cobbler into a small dish, and allow it to cool thoroughly.
2. Cut the apple slices into two or three pieces each for easier chewing, and serve!

FOR HUMANS
1. Top your serving with a healthy sprinkle of cinnamon, and stir to combine throughout.

CINNAMON!

Normally this dish would be made with cinnamon added in step 5, but cinnamon can be dangerous for cats at larger doses, so I advise leaving it out of kitty's share entirely. If you're using individual baking dishes, you can add half of the oat topping to kitty's dish (step 6), then add cinnamon to the remaining topping in the mixing bowl, stir, and top your dish with the rest. If you do this, be sure to mark which cobbler is yours before adding it to the oven (stick a toothpick in yours to be sure you'll remember!).

KITTY NOT INTERESTED?

This is the only non-dairy dessert offered in this book, but if it's not catching your cat's attention and she can handle dairy, try a tiny bit of whipped cream on top to get the ball rolling, or let a spoonful of vanilla ice cream melt on top to mix with the other flavors of the cobbler. You'd probably like this, too!

If you don't like the word "hairball,"
try its official name: bezoar.

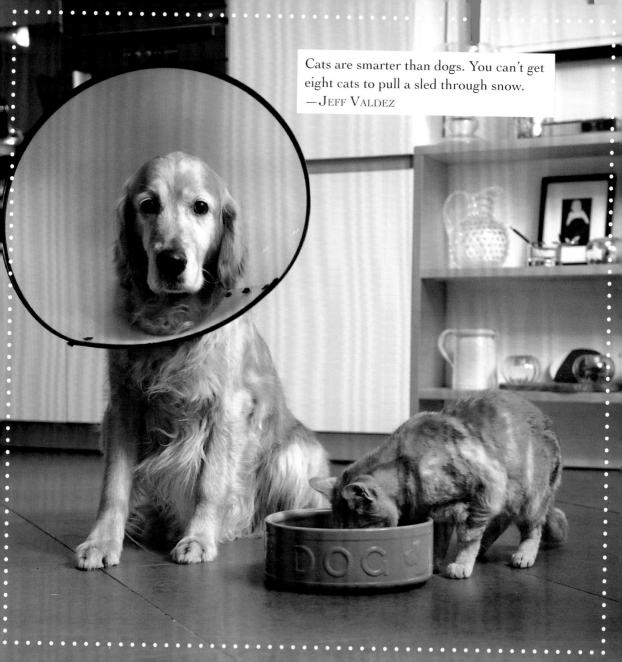

Cats are smarter than dogs. You can't get eight cats to pull a sled through snow.
—JEFF VALDEZ

Indoor cats live an average of three times longer than outdoor cats.

BLUEBERRY PIE À LA MODE

Prepare your favorite crust recipe (or grab some pre-made crusts), but make your own blueberry pie filling from the recipe below. Your cat doesn't need the preservatives in canned filling (and neither do you, for that matter!), and there may be spices or flavorings in there that aren't safe for kitty either.

Ingredients

FOR BOTH
½ cup sugar
½ cup flour
5 cups blueberries
2 piecrusts, prepared
Vanilla ice cream

Preparation

1. Preheat the oven to 450°F.
2. In a large mixing bowl, combine the sugar, flour, and blueberries, and stir to combine.
3. Line a pie pan with a piecrust. Spread the blueberry filling on the first piecrust.
4. Remove any crimping (edges) from the second crust, cut a hole in the center, or a few air slits, and use it to cover the filling. Pinch the crusts together to seal the border around the pie.
5. Bake 30 minutes, or until the crust becomes lightly golden.
6. Cool before serving!

FOR HUMANS
1. When the finished pie is cool, serve a slice for yourself, and top with a scoop or two of vanilla ice cream.

FOR CATS
1. After you've cut a slice for yourself, and some of the filling has leaked out from the rest of the pie, scoop a couple spoonfuls of the filling into a small bowl, and top with a drizzle of softened vanilla ice cream (unless your kitty doesn't tolerate dairy!).

OTHER FRUIT PIES?

Most other fruit pies are not going to be as simple to make for your cat, and may contain ingredients that are dangerous for kitty. Cherry pie filling includes almond extract, many pre-made fillings include cinnamon and nutmeg, the skin and pit of peaches can contain harmful or toxic properties, and so on. Blueberry is your safest, simplest bet!

BROWNING THE PIE

To encourage browning, you can use a pastry brush to spread a thin layer of softened butter over the pie, but you'll want to check the pie a few times during cooking to make sure it's not blackening if you do this!

While still legal in most of the United States, declawing cats is banned in at least twenty-two countries.

Way down deep, we're all motivated by the same urges. Cats have the courage to live by them.
—JIM DAVIS

The human back has 34 vertebrae, but a cat's 53 make it much more flexible.

CHEESE PLATTER

Cottage cheese is often used by cat owners to trick their finicky companions into taking medicine! If your kitty likes dairy and refuses to take her medicine, smash the pill and sprinkle the powder over the cottage cheese in kitty's platter!

Ingredients

FOR BOTH
2–3 semi-hard and/or hard cheeses of your preference (cheddar, Gouda, Monterey Jack, Parmesan)
3–4 medium strawberries

FOR CATS
Cottage Cheese

Preparation

FOR CATS
1. Onto a small dish, shred about ¾ of an inch of each cheese into a separate pile.
2. Add a Tablespoon of cottage cheese.
3. Garnish with a finely chopped strawberry.

FOR HUMANS
1. Slice the remaining cheese and arrange on a platter with strawberries.

SPREADS

Condiments and spreads aren't great for cats, and some popular cheese companions (like fig jelly) can be toxic to them. Feel free to serve anything you love to yourself, but leave kitty's untopped!

The first cat video uploaded to YouTube was "Pajamas and Nick Drake," by YouTube co-founder Steve Chen in 2005. As of this writing, the video still has only 35,000 views, ten years later.

I have studied many philosophers and many cats. The wisdom of cats is infinitely superior.
—HIPPOLYTE TAINE

Why don't cats enjoy as many flavors as humans? It could be partly because humans have about 10,000 taste buds and cats only have about 470.

BANANA FOOL

A fool is a traditional English recipe of whipped cream and blended fruit that's easy to make, and it's a great use of extra fruit you might be trying to use before it goes bad. If you're in a crunch for time, or just feeling lazy, you can purchase whipped topping and fold the fruit right into it.

Ingredients

FOR BOTH
¾ cup heavy whipping cream
¼ cup sugar
2 bananas

Preparation

1. Peel the bananas. In a mixing bowl, mash them with the back of a fork. Leave some small lumps instead of blending to a complete liquid.
2. Add the whipping cream and sugar to a large mixing bowl and whisk until peaks begin to form (time will vary depending on your speed and strength).
3. Fold the mashed bananas into the whipped cream, and chill for 15 minutes in the refrigerator.

FOR CATS
1. Serve two Tablespoons of the fool on a small plate.

MIX IT UP!

You can use any cat-friendly fruits in a fool. Bananas are used here because they're particularly popular with kitties, but feel free to experiment! Just be sure to refer to the list of unsafe foods in the front of the book [see page x] before trying a fruit you're unsure of.

Cats can hear up to two octaves higher than the average human.

The oldest known cat video was either "Professor Welton's Boxing Cats" or "Falling Cat," both produced in 1894, and both accessible on YouTube.

Usain Bolt, the "fastest human," can run up
to 27 mph. A domestic cat can run 30.

A cat determined not to be found
can fold itself up like a pocket
handkerchief if it wants to.
—LOUIS J. CAMUTI

Cat hearts beat nearly twice as fast as human hearts.

COOKING CONVERSION CHARTS

METRIC AND IMPERIAL CONVERSIONS

(These conversions are rounded for convenience)

Ingredient	Cups/Tablespoons/Teaspoons	Ounces	Grams/Milliliters
Butter	1 cup=16 tablespoons= 2 sticks	8 ounces	230 grams
Cream cheese	1 tablespoon	0.5 ounce	14.5 grams
Cheese, shredded	1 cup	4 ounces	110 grams
Cornstarch	1 tablespoon	0.3 ounce	8 grams
Flour, all-purpose	1 cup/1 tablespoon	4.5 ounces/0.3 ounce	125 grams/8 grams
Flour, whole wheat	1 cup	4 ounces	120 grams
Fruit, dried	1 cup	4 ounces	120 grams
Fruits or veggies, chopped	1 cup	5 to 7 ounces	145 to 200 grams
Fruits or veggies, pureed	1 cup	8.5 ounces	245 grams
Honey, maple syrup, or corn syrup	1 tablespoon	.75 ounce	20 grams
Liquids: cream, milk, water, or juice	1 cup	8 fluid ounces	240 ml
Oats	1 cup	5.5 ounces	150 grams
Salt	1 teaspoon	0.2 ounces	6 grams

Ingredient	Cups/Tablespoons/ Teaspoons	Ounces	Grams/Milliliters
Spices: cinnamon, cloves, ginger, or nutmeg (ground)	1 teaspoon	0.2 ounce	5 ml
Sugar, brown, firmly packed	1 cup	7 ounces	200 grams
Sugar, white	1 cup/1 tablespoon	7 ounces/0.5 ounce	200 grams/12.5 grams
Vanilla extract	1 teaspoon	0.2 ounce	4 grams

OVEN TEMPERATURES

Fahrenheit	Celcius	Gas Mark
225°	110°	¼
250°	120°	½
275°	140°	1
300°	150°	2
325°	160°	3
350°	180°	4
375°	190°	5
400°	200°	6
425°	220°	7
450°	230°	8

ACKNOWLEDGMENTS

My first thanks go to Jonathan Green for the very idea of this book, which started as a joke and turned into a reality.

Next to Melissa Guerriero who immediately divined the adorable title when she heard the concept.

Endless thanks to Michele Florence for bringing Lucy into my life and trusting me with her care. Lucy is my salvation many days, and I always think of how lucky I am that she chose us when Lucy needed a new home.

Naturally, thanks to Lindsey Breuer for sharing my love of kitties and being excited to edit this book. And, of course, for putting up with my crazy schedule during the process!

Finally, thanks always to R. Kurt Osenlund. For designing this cover, for assisting with some photos, for being Lucy's other loving father, and for everything I couldn't possibly find ways to express.

Lucy would like to thank all of the above people, and the inventor of ice cream.